わたしの ヒロシマ

MY HIROSHIMA

Junko Morimoto

Hiroshima is the town of my memories. It is surrounded
by green mountains and looks towards the sea. Through
it flow seven beautiful rivers.

COLLINS

I was the smallest in our family. There was my father and mother, my brother and two elder sisters.

Sometimes I liked to be alone. I would stay at home and draw many things — all day I would draw, it was what I loved most.

I had many friends but my best friends were Fumi and Haruko. We played lots of games — our favourite was "Oranges and Lemons".

Summertime was fireworks time.
It was fun going with my family to
watch the beautiful colours and
patterns as they burst overhead.
They looked so large and high
above the bridge where we stood.

I didn't like going to school. Every morning I would hold
tightly to my brother's jacket and follow behind him.

My teacher wore glasses with heavy, black frames. I liked
him best when he taught us painting.

In the winter of my fourth year at school, a big war
started.

As I grew up, the world around me changed a lot. By the time I reached high school I had to wear special clothes, because the war our country was in influenced everything.

There were fewer and fewer goods in the shops.
Everyone had to spend their summer holidays doing
military exercises.

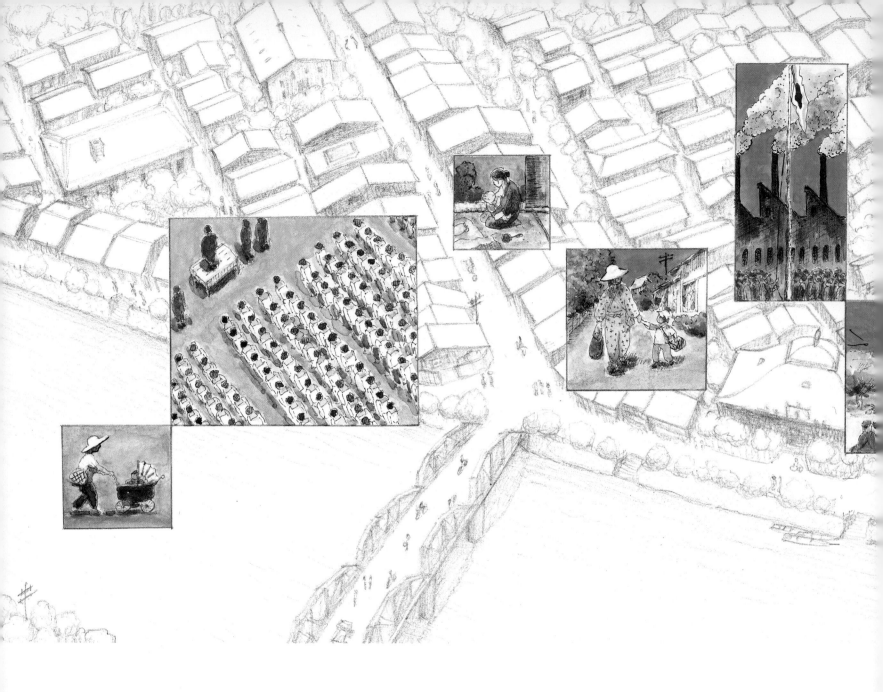

8.15 AM   AUGUST 6   1945

The people of Hiroshima had just begun their day's work. Suddenly, the sirens sounded, warning that a plane was approaching, but the sirens soon stopped and everyone went about their work.

This day I had a pain in my stomach and was not going to school. My sister and I were in our room talking.

I thought I heard the sound of a plane, but it seemed a
long way off and very high up.

I was hit by a thunderous flash and
an explosion of sound.

My eyes burnt — everything went
black. I held my sister.

Everything faded away — I thought I
was dying.

I woke up. I was alive. But my home was completely destroyed.

When I crawled outside, I found that the whole of Hiroshima was destroyed. Everything was blown away, torn apart. Everything was burning.

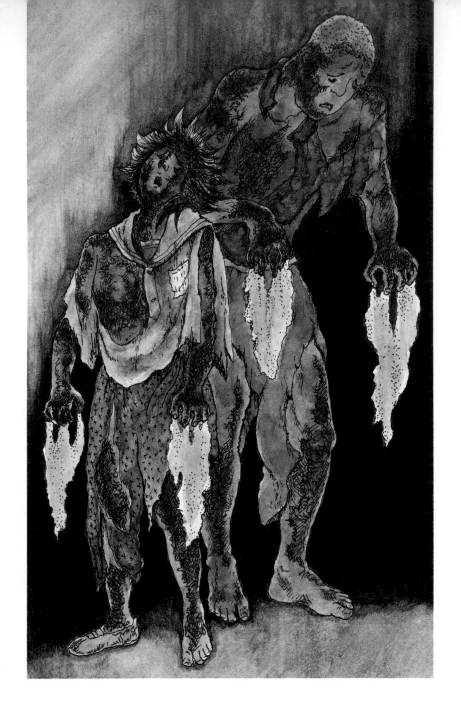

The banks of the river were crowded with people,
everyone wanted to be near the water.

I saw a girl with her skin hanging from her nails.

There was a child, screaming, trying to wake-up her
dead mother.

I was very lucky, my family were all alive and we were together, sheltering in a cave.

Father's face was badly burnt and swollen. My brother's back was full of pieces of glass from the window he was sitting beneath. My eldest sister had her teeth sticking through her lip, she had been using chopsticks.

We watched as hundreds and hundreds of people escaped from burning Hiroshima, under the strong sunlight of summer.

Every school became a hospital for the badly injured.
I heard people screaming and moaning in pain, and
there was a horrible smell of burnt skin.

Many people died, one after another. Their bodies were
taken to the school's playing field and burnt.

Several days later we heard the announcement
that the war was over.

Half a year passed.

The students who had survived went back to
their schools. From the dirt of the burnt
earth I took an aluminium lunch box with
burnt, black rice inside. I found the bones of
many of my friends.

Many, many years have passed and I have returned to my school again.

It is still a miracle that I survived.

All I see now is clean white ground and peaceful images of young students, who are just like I was so long ago.

© Illustrations and text: Junko Morimoto 1987
First published in 1987 by William Collins Pty Ltd. (Sydney)
Reprinted 1988
Typeset by Keyset Phototype Pty Ltd.
Printed by Mandarin Offset, H.K.

British Library Cataloguing-in-Publication Data available

ISBN 0 7322 4813 2

LET ALL THE SOULS HERE REST IN PEACE,
FOR WE SHALL NOT REPEAT THE EVIL.